KIRKSVILLE

KIRKSVILLE

POEMS BY BOB MIELKE

Donald Books
New York   Shelter Island, NY

Published by Donald Books
donaldbooks.com
310 W. 99th Street, No. 503
New York, New York 10025

©2012 by Bob Mielke. All Rights Reserved.
ISBN 978-0-578-10434-8
First printing April 2012.

Library of Congress Cataloging-In-Publication Data
Mielke, Bob, 1954 -
Kirksville: Poems by Bob Mielke
p. cm.
ISBN 978-0-578-10434-8 (pbk)
I. Title.

No part of this publication may be reproduced or transmitted in any form without first obtaining the explicit permission of the copyright holder.

For Jim Barnes, of course, *il miglior fabbro*,
but also for Kirksville and all
who've resided in it,
however briefly . . .

KIRKSVILLE

Contents

The Confederate Army Field Hospital..1

Central Cab..2

La Fuente, Baltimore Street..3

On Leisure Drive...4

Cemetery Theater..5

Fireworks Over Marshall's Farm...6

From Normal Street...7

Upstairs at Too Talls Two..8

Finding Mark Spitzer..9

From the Deck: Salamander Grill...10

Meeting Susan S. at the Traveller's Hotel..11

At the English Senior Seminar Conference......................................12

Looking for Sontag's Ghost at Toons...13

Triolet for Karl..14

Woodwinds Apartments..15

Brashear Park (Within a Budding Grove)..16

Madrigal for the Gardener..17

Usinger's Sausage..18

Used Books and Unicorns...19

Vandals...20

Three Deaths..21

Magruder Hall Planetarium..25

2404 North East Street...26

The Trip to Bountiful..27

Steve Davis' Lament..28

At the Du Kum Inn..29

Washington Street Java Company...30

A Lampshade Made of Human Skin..31

No Direction Home..32

Around the Square..33

Near Arnie's House...34

Milwaukee Idyll...35

The Sunken Garden..38

The Sun on Forest Lake...39

Bequest: *Mi Corazon* to RVM...40

Bequest: *Piss Santa* to the Truman Art Gallery................................41

Ballade..42

Cat Memorials...43

Shepard Outsider...44

At the Lake Restaurant...45

At the Student Union Fountain..46

It's Karaoke Night!..47

Dar Williams on the Truman Campus Quad...................................49

In My Library, A Promise..50

Peabody's Pictorials...51

Homage to Paris..52

David Norton's *Police One* in my Media Room...............................53

Baldwin Hall Bridge...54

Touring Forest Lake..55

"Got Any Spare Change?"..56

Down the Hill to Jim's Funeral Pyre..57

All Yesterday's Dinner Parties...58

Invocation and Rodeo	59
Mormons in the Rain	60
Homage	61
The Blue Moon	62
Stormbringer	63
After the Parade	64
Before the Deluge	67
Interlude	68
Ruth Towne's Bell	69
Friday Night Concerts on the Square	70
Aporia	71
Betty Ford Died	72
The Pink Picnic	73
Another American Poet	74
Le Dialogue au Carmel	75
Commemoration	76
One O'clock in the Morning	77
Rod's Way: July 2011	78
Heat Advisory	79
At the Greek Corner	80
Poem on Hemingway's Birthday	81
Departures	82
Midnight in Paris in Kirksville	85
About Bob Mielke	87
Kirksville Bonus Tracks: Q&A with Bob Mielke	89

The Confederate Army Field Hospital

Sherry, pursuing office under the sign
Of the fish and the elephant, owns
An antiques and consignments shop
On this Christ-haunted square. Cerberus
Barks on the stairs where once young men
Were carried up for amputations
And wound-dressings.

Colonel McNeil's army had sluiced
Into the town's center from north and east
While Joseph C. Porter's snipers had claimed
Window vantages from the fleeing citizenry,
Delaying the inevitable by killing 28 and wounding 60.
Return fire claimed 35 and sent 75 up the
Stairs of the old Ivie Hotel—although estimates vary.

An easy date to remember now: August 6, from a
Distant year: 1862. Some historians hint that this date
Also was a military turning point in Missouri's Civil War,
The sapping of Porter's rebel recruitment drive. In 1870,
McNeil, become a Brigadier General, lobbied the legislature
To give Kirksville the state normal school because of
The historical heft of the site. So it came to pass.

The Ivie building hosted by turns the Boston Store
(With adjacent bowling alley and shooting gallery),
J. C. Penney's, Books and Things (Herman Wilson
Quipped "more things than books".) Now it's Sherry's
Domain with all the Jesus a dying confederate soldier
Could ever have desired.

An attendant follows holding a tray, he carries a refuse pail,
Soon to be fill'd with clotted rags and blood, emptied, and fill'd
Again.

I onward go, I stop, contemplating a
"Guide to Christian Publishing" and a big sign
On the top floor of the shop: Howe Bicycles and
Tricycles, 48 Boulevard de Sebastopol,
Paris, illustration of a man on a gargantuan trike,
Chartreuse background, $27.50. Nearby,
Lou Gehrig, Spiderman gaze at me.

Around the corner, where limbs were carefully
Sawed, an empty 2004 Beringer White Zinfandel bottle
On the top shelf (no price tag), troll doll nurses
And a Casper the Friendly Ghost lunch box.
Samaritans threw the amputated limbs out the back window
Into the alley till "a cart load accumulated"—broken parts
From A. T. Still's marvelous man-machine, hidden treasures.

(Violette's *History of Adair County*)

Central Cab

Call Doug if an ice storm
Suddenly arrives while you were
Checking e-mail—or if a blizzard
Outstrips your footwear. Or
Maybe you've just been drinking
A little and don't want to
Lose your license.

Lacking a car, I go everywhere
In his cab: Hy-Vee, Walmart,
The baseball diamonds north of town,
Forest Lake, the Du Kum Inn,
Occasionally the Uptown Café or
The Amtrak station or local airport.
Doug's rates are reasonable and his
Service reliable and fast as feasible.

If you're new to the area, his rich
Country brogue can be hard to pick up.
But it's worth the effort to catch it
Over the radio's squawk of Cardinals baseball,
"Party line" swapmeets or oldies radio
(Oliver's "Jean".) Doug has tales of
Gardening, dogs, driving a dairy truck
For many years. He may even tell you
About the psycho who overpaid him, then
Pistol-whipped him into the emergency room,
All the while cajoling him to "Relax. Relax."

Best of all, you may share your cab
With people you'd never otherwise meet:
Trailer park residents, fast food workers,
A guy just out of a Kansas City jail
Who took a swing at a cop
Who suddenly woke him up
As he slept on the hood of a car
At a KC rock festival.
The missed week may cost him his Walmart job.
But you have no worries if
You leave the driving to Doug.

La Fuente, Baltimore Street

1. Any Given Saturday

Guests from St. Louis
Say it's better Mexican
Than they can get.
After a Friday night's debauch,
You just can't beat the huevos
Con chorizo, the fresh sausage
Gritty without gristle
On the corn tortilla.

Top it with their homemade
Hot sauce, an orangish-yellow
Blast of serpentine fire to the palate.
Get started with a margarita or
An ice-cold bottle of Dos Equis
Or Negra Modelo. After all,
Saturday night will bookend this brunch.

2. 2008: Bastille Day

Back from Iowa City and the
Somber traces of the catastrophic
Floods, we prop Arnie's sticks in a
Corner and have a real Mexican
Monday. Service seems skewed somehow.

Margarita, no salt, gets reversed by the
Harried waiter still grappling with his
Second tongue. The platter with tortillas,
Pico de gallo, sour cream, guacamole,
Rice and refried beans arrives ten
Minutes after Barb's vegetarian fajitas skillet.

No sweat, though: each bite is
Muy delicioso. No one's in any rush.
We're just glad to be here, reprieved
From surgeries, natural disasters and revolutions.

On Leisure Drive

A disproportionate number of the town's
Authors elect to live there, believing
All too much in the power of the name
And perhaps expecting even better sidestreets:
Pleasure Circle, Contentment Lane.
A subdivision of tacit rewards, deserved.

Mark Spitzer and Robin Becker started
It all with their backyard wedding.
The muses were invoked with fireworks
And Western's barbecue and beef briskit,
Then held curious by the mounted
Fish trophies, the morbid child safety posters.

(Fruits from years of yardsale gleanings)
And a nearly operational fallout shelter
Under the patio, replete with blast door:
The ultimate attraction of this populuxe
Masterpiece. The muses stayed awhile
In the couple's casual po mo salon.

Other writers moved onto the street: the
Savile Row suitcoated German prof who gives away
Articles on idealist philosophy to Oxford online
Bought a split level two doors up.
Once past the gargoyle on the steps,
Rod and Susan would regale you with strong
Gin and tonics, soufflés, bouillabaisse and macaronic chat.

Now much is ashes. Another writer bought
The address Mark and Robin were renting, helping to
Send them on an odyssey of addresses;
My gal dumped me, so I don't walk over there
For exercise much anymore; Susan kicked Rod out.
On a hot spring day, Patrick and I moved him out under
The watchful eye of the sheriff neighbor. Leisure
Came later at Minn's bar: it had left the street
Tucked away in a box with Rod's pipe collection.

Cemetery Theater

Our true Day of the Dead comes in July.
Under the brightest green-yellow canopy
We file down the cobblestone paths to meet
Illustrious residents of Kirksville's past,
Poised to hail us alongside their tombstones.

Andrew and Mary Still exhort provocatively by
A real skeleton; Rose Reiger talks of
Births and hardships and her stolid Lutheranism;
John and Bethea Aitken reiterate their struggles
In the mining town of Novinger with Irish accents.

A seven year old, Harvey Harley Dockery,
Hangs from a commodious branch over his grave,
Then jumps to remind us that kids are
Buried here too. His playful spirit jams the
Gears on the golf cart, ripping up the cemetery
Lawn, driving the cart up an embankment
And nearly throwing Arnie and the driver out.

Such are the risks of those who flirt with the dead.
John and Mary Porter, fortunately, are more
Gracious—as they should be, given the number of
Streets in town named after their offspring.

We end our sepulchral tour by encountering
Harvey Dix, the first Union casualty in
Adair County; then John Kent, a
Confederate private who was executed in a
Mass shooting after the Battle of Kirksville.
Both too young, they seem to get along now
In the blue and grey uniforms, side by
Side, in the communion of the deceased.
Yet the grave marker for the mass burial of the
Rebels who faced the firing squad warns those who might read:
Deo Vindice. The wind sloughs our sweat with a slight breeze.

Fireworks Over Marshall's Farm

The last day in June. Once again,
Guests from Arizona visit to exploit
The "anything goes" fireworks accessibility of
Adair County. Blow up anything sub-nuclear;
Just stop at 11 PM. Jimmy warms

Up the crowd with "I Am the Walrus"
On saxophone, its European police blare sounding to
Cold War survivors like an air raid siren.
Jimmy proceeds to the small materiel:
The 10-shot-for-a-nickel roman candles,
The penny bottle rockets, the buzz bombs that
Go anywhere before loudly exploding—
Which prove to be the most hazardous fireworks
Of the evening: we are showered with flaming hot kibble.

Then it's on to the big stuff: "Wake the
Neighbors," giant Black Cat grand finales
That fill the night with amethyst, jade,
Indigo, amber, sapphire. "The Curse of the
Pharaoh" shoots up a blazing fountain, then
Fires some aerial displays and reports:
Orientalism at its finest from the sellers at the
Shrine Club. We reserve a special place
In our hearts for the nuclear-themed munitions.
Like "Little Boy #5" with its incongruous
Illustration from Operation Plumbbob, shot
Priscilla, at the Nevada Test Site:
A greenish-white-red fountain with explosions.

Best of all is the "Radioactive" series
Of mortars: 18 in all for three launchers
(They wear out from the heat). Number 16
Shoots heavenward, bursts into a myriad
Array of white points of light which
Gradually dim away. But for three or

Four magic seconds, the viewers cannot
Discern where the firework's illumination ends
And the night sky with stars begins—so
Seamless is the image. We feel touched by a
Vision, a miracle of pyrotechnics. We gasp in
Silence until the jokes begin about psychedelic
Dosings. Then we hear Tom Marshall's sheep
Bleating, glad for the lull in our blessed apocalypse,
And, perhaps, the scintillation and flicker
Of the canopy of the Pleroma.

From Normal Street

I can't see more than two blocks
in any direction. The orange street light
on the corner flickers on and off
in response to the repeated lightning strikes
which it reads as daybreak.

The sheets of water cascading off
   my rain gutter flash like tiny diamond
facets in the stroboscopic effects
of the electrical storm. The street
is a tumid river. It's been raining since dawn.

Now it's late evening, and the police
   cars have shut down Baltimore Street
because Normal has flooded. Their
strobes are multicolored—red, white and blue.
Cars, SUVs and pickups pass my house in a

soft wet parade. I sit on my porch
and sip Eagle Rare whiskey:
television is not only too risky
but vastly inferior entertainment.
One lone guy stumbles toward the KFC on the corner.

My tin kitchen roof is leaking and
filling utility buckets and salad bowls.
My phone lines have gone to static. This is
a relentless soaking. But the bourbon
tastes like heaven, which has opened up on us.

Upstairs at Too Talls Two

Kevin Fitzpatrick orders another pitcher
of Budweiser for P. J. O'Rourke,
who chats and flirts with
communication majors after his big
lecture on "Holidays in Hell."

Vincent Price (signed), Greta Garbo
and Marlon Brando look on as our
waitress, a curly-headed blonde
in black miniskirt and
barbershop quartet striped top
(the restaurant's uniform
for that hybrid retro look)
pours the frothy brew
into our frosty mugs.

P.J. is one charming conservative,
a seemingly odd fit at Rolling Stone.
He regales us with tales
of wacky Hunter S. Thompson and the casual
Reagan White House. Nachos arrive.

O'Rourke's kind of journalist invites
groupies: trysts are planned, and
a return visit for bow season
where P. J. can also encounter
turkey hunter Ted Nugent.

Everyone is getting nicely buzzed.
O'Rourke enjoys his casual fame
and the luscious fruits it delivers.
Spring dreams enrich the beer,
which in turn accelerates
what will suffice for intimacy
on this April night.

Finding Mark Spitzer

Maggie arrives for Paris movie night
Little expecting my cinematic curve ball,
Last Tango in Paris, for feminists a fright,
Shown to commemorate my cursing call
Under Pont Hakim Bey in Paris' afternoon light
With Maggie, homage to Brando's nihilistic squall.
But there's much more: fellatio and butter
And mooning. Still Maggie does not mutter.

Film over, we try to find a party
For the English grad students, hosted by Mark Spitzer
On Overbrook Drive; acting like a smarty
I think I don't need a map to locate this mixer.
After driving around fruitlessly, with a hearty
Sigh I resign myself to consult a convenience store fixer.
What he tells us makes little sense,
So we abandon our quest with little pretense.

Instead, plan B, we head over to Rod's
Where he's drinking red wine with Alci.
When Maggie enters the room, the blind god
Lets his arrows fly every which way.
Maggie accepts a glass, resting her chic mod
Apparel next to me on a comfy settee.
Small talk is exchanged, Rod and Maggie met before;
But neither can anticipate all that's in store.

So it goes: even August Strindberg
In Berlin's Black Pig could rage and rant
About woman the whore and the foul demiurge
Yet still get remarried for all of his cant
When little August had a persistent urge—
Drives far from the imperatives of Kant.
We love whom we will, we love whom we must,
We go somewhere else if first plans go bust.

From the Deck: Salamander Grill

Opting to dine outside, we clamber up
canvas seats so tall we have
to use the side bar near the base: a throwback
to days of the high chair where we once supped.

The view from the deck is remarkable:
a span of manicured grass, a hotel pool,
semis belching soot in the far distance—
a crazed pastoral to grace our table.

Gumbo, jambalaya, crawfish etouffeé
in large portions need Tabasco
to transport us back down to Rue Royale:
a journey often made down the adjacent highway.

The mudbugs, shrimp and andouille
are not from around here, that's clear;
those trucks in the distance must have borne
them to us over many a crooked mile.

The sun descends, mosquitoes emerge
and the cicadas begin their nightly dirge
for distant relatives dumped in the roux;
"*Laissez les bon temps roulez*," they seem to say,
"but only for you. We have musical work to do."

Meeting Susan S. at the Traveller's Hotel

She comes down to the lobby, shock
of white hair run through all the black
and taller than me, full of talk
already, admiring the tracks
that run by this railroad hotel:
Susan likes this place where we dwell.

She keeps striking beauty with age:
no longer the girl in Warhol's
screen test, she has turned a new page
writing a tale of volcanoes.
The prairie sunset blazes red;
we walk to shops, letting her lead.

She fills my arms with Janacek's
string quartets and Lampedusa's
Leopard, praising this last with manic
joy—I cannot fight this Medusa.
"A central text for Europe's soul!"
Purchases in hand, food's our next goal.

At Minn's, colleagues' palaver stuns
Susan, whose riposte is to say
that sarcasm is to be shunned
by serious thinkers, that they
should rather love where they can teach
and live, not wish for what's out of reach.

At the English Senior Seminar Conference

Fortified with a double latte to cut last night's gin,
we lumber to the Georgian Room early Thursday morning.
Alanna's tough lines channel Bukowski's
boozy muse and resurrect the room's drinking habits:
her reading ends with a flourish, applause and a grin.

Then Emily gives us Hillary S & M,
the candidate in drag dancing at "Bear Night"
in "The Oval Orifice," a transgressive treat
that exposes the millennial generation's deep ambivalences
about this dragon lady who underwhelms them.

Pressure drops with Marie's ventriloquized whine,
a prose piece exploring Bukowski's women victims
who still can't help lovin' that man:
the words are prolix and lack sense description,
making it hard to empathize with a voice of that kind.

Finally Deborah dares to play it slightly mad
with overhead transparencies of vaginas and pricks,
Kathy Acker's postmodern postfeminist tricks
which please the trendies and *épater* the hicks.
We think: three out of four ain't bad.

Chett adjourns the session, we shuffle out the door;
But the next presentation on absinthe makes us eager for more.

Looking for Sontag's Ghost at Toons

Prince's "Pussy Control" drives my feminist cohorts
down the metal scaffolding and out the bar;
only football players and sorority drunks are
apt for this mating dance. I sip my well
bourbon and Coke and recall when this was

Tony D's Corral with live bands instead of deejays.
On a request from Susan Sontag, I got up
and snarled "Jailhouse Rock" with the country
cover group, channeling the old impersonator days.
Then we danced to "I Don't Want to Spoil the Party,"

which made Susan sad somehow. We sat down
and I inquired. "I knew John and Yoko. I used to
always see them at parties. They were such good people."
She sighed, and a tear ran parallel to her mane.
A cowboy asked her to dance, as cowboys always do

when they see a sad beauty: "The Tennessee Waltz."
Susan towered over his black ten-gallon hat, sexy punk
lesbian grandma. I cherish her still with my bourbon.
Now I dream of electronic quartets played using radios, dating
Marilyn Monroe, Wyoming shootouts—an almost unsung hero.

Triolet for Karl

My growing woodpile lays unused,
lacking your desire for a fire.
Where once birthday limbs fell so bruised,
my growing woodpile lays—unused
to your new absence unexcused:
surely your ghost seeks out this pyre.
My growing woodpile lays, unused,
lacking you, desire for a fire.

Woodwinds Apartments

In the center of the complex
the pool glistens, inviting sex
of a watery variety;
the grounds are spare and quite vacant—
well-tended by boys truculent.
I recall all past gaiety:

Christiane stirs her rich brown roux
for a dinner party that's never through;
Tim passes out at his own wedding
five minutes after the vows
and our premature applause—
assuring all they'll be no bedding

this wedding night. He looks a fright!
Still we pass hors d'oeuvres with great delight
—cheese platters, cucumber sandwiches—
over his reclining form, sure
his bride will have much to endure
now that she's snared this crazy Manwich.

All long since gone, still great souls live
here: Hena, who'd happily give
you all her time with vindaloo
spiced to taste, or author Obi
whose African treats please readily . . .
And after dinner, a poem or two.

Brashear Park (Within a Budding Grove)

Jennifer and I walk Adrian over
to the wading pool near my home. The grass
flares bright summer green-yellow,
chlorophyll-drenched. We set up metal chairs
and blankets, handing out fruit rolls
and lathering sun lotion over us all.

A gush of young mothers arrive, clad in bikinis
of every rainbow hue, lush body types
ranging from Henry Moore statues through
Rubens to Modigliani and anorexic Giacometti:
a broadband spectrum to entice and snare
any libido. I'm the only guy here, and the oldest.

Then the lifeguard arrives, brunette Venus
with a trashy paperback brightly colored.
Her watch is more about stopping
splashing games than rescuing the drowning.
It's a good gig. Still she eyes my odd
presence, as does every passing poodle and mutt.

Adrian plays with some nearby kids; snacks
are shared. A thirtyish gal smiles
appreciatively at my pseudo-paternal
presence. Snodgrass, Commander Cohen,
you should have been here: you would have
appreciated this festival of youth and fertility
at the kiddie conclave, Nature's spavined dance.

Madrigal for the Gardener

T.J. arrives every day with compost, inquiries, advice—
adrift on an economy bollixed up far away,
although freestyle frisbee seldom paid a bill.

He plants tomatoes, sweet basil, rosemary, mint,
Italian red peppers, and the fiery habanero
we have somehow learned to cherish for its blistery heat—

Scoville-pegged off the charts. Once I jammed
with him weekly, an endless keyboard arabesque
of "Space" that threatened to become marijuana melody.

His longtime girlfriend dumped him, he needs the dough;
he has the knack for making it all grow.

I watch with interest, the economy's beat:
I may depend upon his labor's fruits to eat.

Usinger's Sausage

a box on my front porch sits
with happy elves on its side,
cold to the touch with the melting dry ice;
I carry it gingerly inside.

The contents exude my Milwaukee home:
liverwurst, mortadella, Great Lakes cheddar cheese,
beerwurst, summer sausage, Grebe's bakery rye,
yachtwurst and more—all guaranteed to please.

Each bite like Proust's madeleine,
Suds City memories come flooding back:
the triumphs and tragedies, death and loss,
the friends I have, the loves I lack.

Though winter's cold the sausage warms
through the odd alchemy of preparation;
the happy elves are anxious to know
that their work has reached its destination.

Used Books and Unicorns

I enter Shirley's shop for the unicorn hunt:
they won't come if you seek them, there's the rub.
She has choice books, but not the ones you seek.

I looked in vain for Tolkien, Delany, Ballard,
scanning the shelves until I got frazzled—
vain explorations for many a week.

It was a better bookstore to visit
with a friend who couldn't resist
encouraging you to expand your reading:

for she had curiosities aplenty
culled from estate sales all over,
so good discoveries would be made from heeding

that friendly advice. She carried especially fine travel
tomes: southern France, China, Native American marvels
now sit on my shelves, some day to be read.

Now Shirley's in Denver, the store's closed,
she's living with Alzheimer's, oddly disposed
for a woman in love with memory and words.

The new owners just wanted the space
and sent off her stock to our recycling place,
then even burned the rest of the books: absurd!

So all we have now is Hastings, a chain bookstore
that even serendipity seems to abhor.
But thanks to Amazon, things aren't so bleak.

Vandals

Walking to the square
past the boarded-up sushi
joint, I read its wall:

on the yellow wood I see
some "Ellaphunx" graffiti

sprayed in black with red
gang tags superimposed on
top of the slogan.

All who pass by the bold sign
wonder if Kirksville's in decline.

Outside of town on
a former railroad bridge reads
"Keep your pimp hand strong!"

Next to it in another scrawl
"poseur" answers—an apt call.

Country kids want to be
ghetto, form gangs in their hood:
but paint's all they have.

If anyone did serious wrong,
neighbors would out them ere long.

Three Deaths

1. Milwaukee, 1976

John called me on a
Saturday afternoon, his voice
quaking with nervous laughter:
"Peter's jumped off the 35th Street
viaduct. He came by my house
wanting to buy heroin; all I had
was acid. Now he's done it."

"It" was a quasi-scientific
quest: Peter wanted to
burn out his reticular
activating system with LSD—
to level all sensation.
Why? I never asked. I barely
comprehended this ambitious dream
of the professor's son.

He tripped and tripped,
catatonic, while blue collar
buddies burned him with cigarettes
or put ice cubes behind his eyeglasses:
trying to see if anyone was home.

Joy had fled for him, it seemed,
along with Veronique, the French exchange
student who requested
Tom Jones's "She's a Lady"
but settled for King Crimson's *Islands*.
Peter's sand table of dayglo
war games with Nazi tanks and dinosaurs
lay in neglect: the jig was up.

At the funeral service, Curtis Pethke
battered a "jagoff" Coke machine
during the memorial until a beverage was
rendered. We threw Dr. John's
goofer dust on the grave to
the puzzlement of all:
Peter's weird friends.

When the sorrow settled, the parents
invited us over for reminiscences
and remembrances. I got a blue

notebook of drawings and sketches.
Another drawing predicted how he
looked after the plunge: one
glaring black eye through all the bandages.

At Fred's wedding, decades later,
John apologized. I wasn't sure for what,
but I accepted. It all made
sense when I taught *Women in Love*
this last semester: some earnest
interactions by nature are deathly.
We pretend not to see it coming,
but that's macho youth's closure,
existential musical chairs
resolving nothing.

2. Durham, 1979

After pulling a night shift at the Duke library,
I came home to find a message from Greg
in Milwaukee to call—urgent. He tells me
Van has died, self-asphyxiated in his station
wagon in a garage in Iowa City.

They found evidence of a whirlwind
trip to Milwaukee: hotel receipts,
bookstore bags. Then a brisk jaunt back
and the carbon monoxide. Why?

The son of a car dealer in Lowden, Iowa,
Van was a genius boy: out of high school at fifteen,
B.A. from Dalhousie at eighteen, M.A. at nineteen.
Too much too fast. At age twenty-one, he failed
his Duke doctoral oral prelims because he wanted to
discuss George Gissing instead of Charles Dickens.

Then our friendship changed from just expensive wines,
Van's Indian cooking and Peter Maxwell Davies
platter sessions on his elaborate stereo. "Bob,
come over. I've slit my wrists. I want you
to bandage them up. My parents are flying in."
He always went the "wrong" way—sideways.
So I'd alternate putting on Johnson & Johnson's
cream, gauze and surgical tape with
stirring the lentil curry.

Back in Iowa, he remained more

than half in love with easeful death:
I became his impromptu suicide hotline.
Believe me, I know every angle
to persuade you to keep on living from
"life has loveliness to sell" to
"think of the survivors."
But trust me, success is not guaranteed.

Why Milwaukee? A last valentine to me
from a guy who tried to be straight
but couldn't (he even had an older girlfriend)
to a guy who tried to be gay
but really couldn't switch either.
(Van always did like Malcolm Lowry.)
Duke revised its doctoral grilling later
to remove the stench of a body count.
Like Emerson sez, "An institution
is the lengthened shadow of one man."
("Self-Reliance")

3. Kirksville, 2008

Friday cocktails at Woody's are interrupted
by Dereck moaning "No! NO!" to his
cellphone interlocutor. Karl did not outlive Jesus.
Student, grad student, teacher, friend,
social director, walking party, pyro: Karl.

He had his usual breakfast of a Slim Jim
and a Mountain Dew, went to teach high school,
felt some indigestion and pain. The school nurse
sent him home; he went to the store for
some Alka-Seltzer, lay down and passed.

My porch became a spontaneous wake
with absinthe and the last summer drinks
of summer. Even those who never met him shared
our grief. Like Lester Bangs said about Elvis,
it's as if someone said there'd be
no more cheeseburgers. Karl was
a vital force, a food group of the soul.

At the memorial service in St. Louis,
at Trinity Lutheran, where he got married

two years before, our stories
transcended the more sedate tales
we heard at the Bevo Mill reception
from the safer family members:
friends knew a LOT more—

Of nuclear missile silo spelunking
near Roswell, of passing out amidst
the bamboo in Yumi's crisis garden,   (Carl Martin)
of bright plastic mermaids dumped into
an aquarium tank, of Scottish-inflected rants:
"There's no teetotalling in Davy Jones's locker!"

Jess, the widow, blew a large black glass
urn to contain his abundant ashes.
Where some see a spire pointing upward,
I detect an ICBM: even in heaven
Karl can pack a wallop. He smiles
at me through the wise eyes of his infant son
Elliot. Karl inhabits Kirksville like mojo mist,
the genius of this place.

No one can get to Kirksville,
really, except through him.
You have to climb on Karl's blue
school bus, join the world's smallest
St. Patrick's Day parade on Elson street
and throw out beads and swag to the town's
denizens. Then, only then . . .
(Damn everything but the circus.)

The bottles roll on the dorm roof in the Winston-Salem
wind.
Can a tiki weep? Or smile? Or laugh?

Magruder Hall Planetarium

After a walk down the curving ramp
past the named commemorative bricks,
we come in by the neon lamps
into the unfinished planetarium's thick
walls. In the dark of its amphitheater seating
I find a place to watch the proceedings.

We learn of sustainability, riding the rails;
taste the locavore delights of our eatin' Eden.
The greening of our campus is discussed in detail
and how better water quality is needed.
When I leave by a side door into bright sun
I shudder to think how much needs to be done.

At least there's art to mitigate the pain
of all the suffering we've brought to Earth:
on a good day beauty helps explain
to the cosmos humanity's worth.
But do our good deeds tip the scale
enough to counter all the ways we fail?

2404 North East Street

Thursday morning. Marie asks me
in the workroom if I've heard news
about Tom, Spanish retiree.

A woman was crying on his
front steps; then next day at the bar
Laura said that someone saw his

covered body being removed.
On Saturday night I had to
call the KPD who informed

me in a shaky tone that Tom
had been dead for a while—
the news reverberated like a bomb.

Conquistador of vowels and
purveyor of Pisco, macho master
of "La Cucaracha," had penned

his own obituary with
careful foregrounding of Princeton,
an honorable retirement: pith.

Tales surfaced of potlatch freebies
distributed to the neighbors
the week before—kind of creepy.

Family vetoed memorial
services: one news e-mail, then silence,
leaving these words sole testimonial.

The Trip to Bountiful

Where were you born here, Geraldine?
Child of an itinerant man

of medicine, just passing through—
country doctors know what to do

to save a farmer's life or two.
You aspired to find better views.

Smoking hashish with Paul Newman
in Florida, sensual man,

sweet bird of youth to comfort you:
bed-ridden, faded ingénue.

You always yearned for something just
out of reach, irrecoverable, past?

Maybe it's still here in Kirksville:
the *recherche du temps perdu*, full.

Steve Davis' Lament

May 2010

I saw Graceland,
beheld the man
reverentially.

Back in the 'ville
I vowed to thrill
impressionally.

Priscilla sewed
a jumpsuit bold
quite faithfully.

"Suspicious Minds"
on dawn's drive time
gave listeners glee.

I rocked the throng
a thousand strong
ecstatically.

Then found my thrill
at Blueberry Hill
annually.

Don't ever ask
about this mask
painstakingly

worn every day
to evoke E.
eternally.

At the Du Kum Inn

Black and tans take off the spring chill.
The Literary Society holds forth
on politics, art, movies, academic affairs.
Jerry orders a double Laphroaig
when Mattie returns with more beers.

I first came here in eighty-six
with Sam Houston's great grandniece in tow.
Our plane ran out of oil and nearly crashed;
stranded, we explored to and fro
until we found this place to get smashed.

Kim whooped it up, danced on the chairs,
shot pool and talked of working for Streisand
(she obtained vintage clothing for the stars.)
We planned to raise horses and work the land:
promises rather bold even for bars.

She never came to the osteopathy school,
dropped me for a poolside seventeen year old.
In my attic I have her photos still—
a reminder that some who glitter can be cold.
Still it all turned out pretty well.

Just one of many ghosts who haunt these rooms;
visiting poets, deceased profs, Flogging Molly.
Their atoms mingle with our brews
like Shakespeare said in Hamlet's melancholy.
So come on in. Tell us the news.

Washington Street Java Company

Under the historic bas-relief of the ceiling,
warmed by a double latte and general good feelings,
I watch the anonymous parade of beauty:
a woman I just passed by on the street
for instance, dressed in urban formal preparation for some duty
I cannot fathom without being indiscrete.

She too is alone, escaping from the burgeoning heat,
pulling out books and a notepad at her seat—
perhaps knowing of her gift for life's feast.
My office sticker says "Trust Women;" I also
trust beauty, Cixous' laughing medusa.
Perhaps it's conditioning, but certain forms glow
in their own heavenly light like the Mona Lisa.

For that gal it was Da Vinci's *sfumato*,
the blurred paint round the lips that beguiles us so:
we never know for sure what she's thinking.
Our mood becomes her own by projection
 (if we've had a glass of wine, she's been drinking;
if we feel guilty she shares our introjection).

But how to explain that lass in London,
the long-haired blonde on the bike at the intersection?
She stopped morning time in a quick epiphany:
all looked on her as she slowed her conveyance
to anticipate traffic and pose for all sundry
gazers, a *tableau vivant* of aesthetic dalliance.

Or this maiden here, sipping her tea
and considering something quite seriously.
Can it be wrong to drink her in with my eyes
and my latte? It's surely no sin
or sexist leer that I should apotheosize
this fragile punctuation of life's buzzing din.

A Lampshade Made of Human Skin

Or so tour guides used to say
at the Violette Museum
under Kirk Memorial Building on the Truman campus.

Some GI donated it
after liberating a camp in Eastern Europe—
it's the work of some Nazi artisan.

The shade is bulbous and roughly stitched
with the brown tinge of a makeshift tannery;
the base and stem seem factory made

perhaps putting the lie to the horrific claim.
Where's the provenance? Who did the DNA tests?
Still it looked like an obscene glaring electric eyeball

from one of those alien machines
in *The War of the Worlds* films, or a rapatronic camera's
image of the initiation of a nuclear explosion. It embodied

Walter Benjamin's "aura" and a faint evocation of Ed Gein's taxidermy.
Believe it or not; and if you do,
marvel at humanity's brutality and ingenuity.

Now the museum's moved to the Welcome Center
housed at the old firehouse. The lampshade's gone,
replaced by alumna Jenna Fischer's buttery grin.

No Direction Home

Terri told me a long time ago:
 "If you live here ten years, you'll be a local,
but you'll never be a townie."

Proof that Missouri is a southern state
even this far north: when I resided in
North Carolina, I knew it would take

generations to acclimate. So it is here.
Only in big cities can you have the illusion
of belonging—unless you stay where you were born.

But remember, Hugh of St. Victor said
that the perfect traveller
is the one who is at home nowhere.

Around the Square

You smell the scent of kettle corn
and fresh produce: the air hums
with many voices this afternoon.
You sweat profusely in this fall sun,
perhaps because you shared a joint (hippie bum).
The Red Barn street fair has arrived
bringing music, crafts, art and jive.

You stop to buy some painted saws.
One looks like a painting by Thomas Cole—
Home in the Woods—a favorite because
of fourteen summers on the Reynolda House dole.
Another has a lunker bass taking an underwater stroll;
yet another has the last Indian brave
looking over a cliff with expression grave:

an echo of genocidal fantasies.
But what the heck? You buy all three.
Funny how the arts here hark back to a previous century;
still the bold primary colors are lovely to see
and none of the pieces have the warped piety
of the variations on praying hands
or Jesus carved in wood or painted on sand.

Rounding the corner you meet the woman
you've had a crush on for years.
She's thirty years younger, but you're human,
so you chat with her parents without any fears.
Today seems a day without any cares.
Deadwood's bold blues rock out the street,
providing a soundtrack for carnival treats.

Near Arnie's House

I walked down the rocky alley
path as we've done several nights
post pasta dinners with your dog,
Petunia, who could cause fright
with her barking and mad sallies

at your screen door. We'll walk no more
here: your dog passed on of old age;
you lost that leg, a malignant
tumor removed which turned the page.
I saw you yesterday at death's door.

Now you're gone, rapping with Shakespeare
and Ben Jonson, reunited with
friends and pets (I hope) in that strange
undiscovered country. Our grief
has only just begun to appear.

Why do I stroll this path instead
of traipsing down my Normal Street?
I don't want to meet anyone, it
seems—and yet I do. The old beat
hobbit retiree nods his head

and walks past down the rustic path,
pipe to mouth, a strange harbinger
of uncanny days yet to come.
Rising, I heard my messenger
tell me of your overnight death.

6/2/2010

Milwaukee Idyll

1. The Station at La Plata

We arrive scant minutes
before train time.
We've talked to "Julie,"

the Amtrak roborep
who's given us serial updates
in her pleasing cybervoice

while we've downed (in Kirksville)
a whole bottle of morning chardonnay
to calm Rod's travel jitters.

Alci's ride to the station
is accented by fuzzy
overcast white wine light

and ubiquitous buzz comfort.
We lurch past the prairie
simulacrum into the waiting area.

When we step outside
a highballing freight
evaporates our stupor

and pins us back,
harnessing all the forces
of Aeolus and Boanerges.

2. Southwest Chief

We lurch through the Missouri
countryside, overcast but
verdant from rain's gifts.

Looking for bald eagles,
we cross the Big Muddy
at Fort Madison,

then savor a cheeseburger

in the dining car
with friendly strangers.

More crisp chardonnay
is grabbed from the
lounge car's cooler.

We change trains at
Chicago's Union Station
wafting through the sweaty

bodies to our Hiawatha
service where a Robin Williams
look-and-act-alike

will clown and deliver us
more drinks as he tickles
dour commuters with a feather toy.

3. Three Brothers

After we send shots of
slivovitz back to the kitchen,
the last brother

standing comes to join our table.
Rod compliments him on
the best grilled lamb

he's ever enjoyed. The owner
closes the place so Rod can smoke.
Toasts circle freely

and we hear of genocides,
civil wars, the uneasy Balkans
while we drink away

these painful memories,
leaving only the bounteous moment
of this magic night.

4. Pfister Hotel

We stay on the supposedly
haunted fourth floor: the only ghost,
Biedermeier

furnishings and bibelots by the elevator.
The skyline bar unfurls the harbor to
piano jazz

like a diorama. We sip martinis,
then waken to the squawk of gulls
perched on our roof.

It's Willa Cather's "Paul's Case" for two:
uninterrupted luxury and the best
Bloody Mary

in the cosmos, replete with Usinger's
sausage sticks and a chunky cheddar block:
midwestern paradise!

The Sunken Garden

The crowd assembles in a place where
marriage proposals have been tendered
on bended knee in the arbor:
this midsummer night we come here
to see Shakespeare justly rendered

by Becky Becker's student troupe of
players. You know what show they act
this season under the starry
sky. Costumed nymphs hand out bubble
dispensers for those who want to
become a part of this fey tract.

As if on cue, we blow the soapy
puffs whenever fairies arrive
on the scene, magic accomplices
for Titania and Oberon.
We were not told we must do this,
but we are happy to connive.

The bowered space offers natural ways
to enter and exit for our
nubile cast in diaphanous
apparel. The play's a big smash
with silly mechanicals, fair
maidens and an Egeus dour.

Mystery, mirth, romance, art combine
in this sublime artwork blended
from fairy dust and thespian
youth. We clap long and hard for them
after our revels have ended.

The Sun on Forest Lake

A slight warm spell relieves
the December chill as Mary
and I cavort on the Point
with her French bulldog, Champagne.
Snugly covered in his doggie sweater,
he's willing to endure all weather.

The shoreline's edges have melted,
but a long patch of blue ice
remains in the lake's center on which
hundreds of Canadian geese preen
and mutter, enjoying this weather fine
but knowing they're bound for southern climes.

One goose becomes the leader: his
honking brings some to form a delta
shape with the proud male at its tip.
After much cacophony, the sound recedes
and he slowly takes to the azure sky
causing the rest of his posse to fly.

Champagne stands amazed, too intrigued
to bark. They hover over the lake in formation,
then gradually ascend and bank to the south,
doubling back on their ice-locked kin—
thus inspiring another ground leader to emerge
and remind them of their migratory urge.

Bequest: *Mi Corazon* to **RVM**

Take this heart that seems to flutter
whenever I see you enter
a room—unlike any other

with your almond eyes, calm banter
and million dollar smile. My gaze
confirms you're a great enchanter.

Your sinuous curves belie days
you have surely lived in distant
tropical places. I'm amazed

at how you embrace each instant
while we sip the cool margaritas
at La Pachanga, blessed moment

of bliss, lovely senorita.
Yet it's not tequila goggles
alone that deem you time cheater,

but something else—my mind boggles.
Graced be the man who calls you lover:
you'll bring him the sweetest struggles.

Bequest: *Piss Santa* to the Truman Art Gallery

Being of sound mind if weary
body, I give to the Truman
Art Gallery my own very

original proof of human
ingenuity: "Piss Santa"
by Steve Shepard, a quite fuming

environmentalist ~ can't abide
what BP has done to his
dear Gulf Coast, showing nary a

twinge of guilt. May they drink *their* piss
in perpetuity for that crime.
Steve's work is not at all like this.

His Santa's in corn oil which time
has evaporated, making it
a self-consuming work so fine:

it's piss after all and not shit.
Take this, Truman, in thanks for your
failure to honor a legit

promise for time off when eight years
roll around. I have better gifts
but you shan't receive them, I fear.

Ballade

When I die, scatter my ashes
above the Aioi bridge, where men
once dropped the first a-bomb; the flash
gave Hiroshima endless pain
from which I profit now and then.
I'd like to join the exploited
souls when my time at last must come
on Ota's river of the dead.

Or, if you must, economize by
placing the ashes in an urn
in the Kirksville cemetery
overlooking all those who learn
medicine or liberal arts; turn
a cold eye on my blanched remains
while you labor so hard to earn
your bread and butter through your pains.

Celebrate my life with a drink;
make my service a roaring wake
of any potions you might think
most fittingly your thirst would slake.
Don't be afraid if glass should break.
Stay up until you see sunrise—
a time of day I'd seldom wake
to, preferring my shut-eyes.

Or if the funeral's deluxe,
drink sake, whiskey in Japan;
bring sashimi in by the truck
and toast "konbai!" to this gone man.

Cat Memorials

I've only had a few cats die
on my watch; most slink off somewhere
if you're dumb enough to let them
roam outdoors in a city—even here.
Only two exceptions: Top Cat,
who died of feline leukemia
and FIV, orange tabby—
and black Yusef Komunyakaa.
I held the former as he took
the lethal injection at the
vet's, then penned a memorial
to him at home, distributed
discretely among the right friends.
(He was cremated instantly.)
Yusef had a bad heart, I was told
("don't get too attached to this one,"
the doctor said—what a big laugh).
I found him keeled over one night
after returning from Rod's in
a vinous state. I simply moved
him into the back yard, under
my luxuriant bamboo, and
covered him with the fresh snow fall.
'Twas not a secure grave, alas:
I think raccoons moved his remains
under my porch, then kids found them till
I finally relocated them
in my compost heap. I promise
to mend my ways with my current
four cats: they shall receive fine urns
with their names on them (Heidi,
Merlin, Sylvia, Michael Field),
"To My Friend" inscribed on each one.

Shepard Outsider

Beings emerge from their round craft,
a cross between an egg and sun;
across the bayou waves they waft
hovering like the Chosen One.

Their arrival portends no fun—
although the scene seems rather daft.
Alien harbingers, they come
to take fishermen to their craft.

Some see this painting and must laugh
at the kooky way it's been done:
the glyphs around the landscape apt
evocation of Paul Klee's fun

doodles in "Around the Fish," one
might note, if one liked arty japes.
Steve's colored pencils surely stun
the open eye with silv'ry craft.

The spaceships in starry night waft
over the swamp and bid us come
with the aliens on their craft
to learn how the universe runs
and explore galaxies, adrift
and bewildered on their space raft.

At the Lake Restaurant

Every Halloween Rod and I escape
from the urchins to the lake
(weary of their sparse patronage
when I provide some candy to take).

We do it right with martinis crisp
and *vins blanc et rouge*;
we munch on mozzarella sticks
and toasted ravioli too.

The sun goes down on Forest Lake
when our lobsters and filets arrive:
everything gets dipped in butter
as long as we're alive
(and people that's no jive)—

especially the crackers and rolls
so humble to behold.
Bread shared with a *bon companion*'s
a tale that never gets old.
(At least that's what I'm told
by everyone with soul.)

Our meal then done, gone with the sun,
we have that one last drink
before we have to call Central Cab
and pay more than we think
as back to town we slink
for yet another drink
to keep us in the pink.

At the Student Union Fountain

We take it for granted, a universal
obstacle blocking Pickler Library, Student Union
Building and Magruder Hall.

No statues adorn it: where's Harry S. Truman
adding water to his bourbon
or cradling the mushroom spray

of Bikini Shot Baker? Or Mark Twain
mocking pissing putti, spitting juice
from his Havana cigar?

The fountain's dyed purple for Homecoming
or Graduation—as good as it gets.
It's turned off in winter when it can serve

as an amphitheater for Brother Jed's
clownish take on Christianity—or for
the butterfly flutters of student activism

twenty-first-century style. Mostly it subtly echoes
boom boxes on utility tables
that entice us to neglected concert events

or, when wet, a place for dogs, kids
and beleaguered students to dip their feet;
maybe even cavort, frolic—living naiads!

Still, the fountain offers a *promesse de bonheur*
forcing us to circumnavigate the mundane,
giving us a chance to change our life.

It's Karaoke Night!

Another epic rain
inspires Linda's picks:
"Stormy Weather," "Over the Rainbow."
Her sultry soprano
carries over the hubbub of

moistened chatter. Ron
delivers Queen's "Funny Little Thing
Called Love" before Dereck grooves
on Wall of Voodoo's "Mexican Radio."
A big-bottomed anonymous

showgirl dances on a table,
rocks the house. I want to
marry her then and there.
She taunts a nearby beer lad
with claims of a shared

schooling—no doubt bullshit.
She won't give out her real name.
José wants me to sing, so
I follow up .38 Special's fair gig
by rubbishing Neil Young

(whom I just wrapped a long
chapter about), wailing
Skynyrd, even dropping
the f-bomb to born-again dj
Wendy's consternation.

The big gal assists. Then
Gina kisses me to repay
a drunken compliment
and channels Sarah McLachlan
effortlessly—the whole room's

in the arms of an angel.
Her husband nails Neil Diamond
as always. The jumbo mystery
blonde gets the last word with
Sir Mix-A-Lot, with my help:
fast-rapping and back-bumping

cuz, yeah, baby does have back.
Tonight every note counts:
no slop was served,
everyone's pro-quality.

If you just dropped by
this Du Kum Inn, you'd
wonder what hermetic
consortium was sharing
such musical jokes

on this rainy night,
Jove nodding to Jove,
a rehearsal for an
eternity of song
guided by beer light:

a paradise already glimpsed
by José in Karianne's
unemployed perfect skin
and casual erudition,
a consolidated vision.

Dar Williams on the Truman Campus Quad

Calling the silver moon, the sorceress sings
to her rapt crowd about many things:
of Yoko, New York's Spring Street,
her babysitter so beat
replete with sad flings,

of Elvis catching a wave in heaven
and Daniel Berrigan's activist leaven
(he had no right but for the love of you).
Calling for the moon,

Dar feels our connection with her—
she enjoyed a coed mom's dinner
served in daughter's dorm space
above the place
we hear her
still calling for the silver moon.

In My Library, A Promise

Kirksville, I will never betray
you for another, better clime
though I have encountered many:
Santa Fe, Marrakech one time,
also Paris, London, sublime
Haiti, forty-eight states I've seen—
New Mexico's my favorite one.

You deserve a loyal bard here
so I will stay if just because
you need a close eye, an apt ear
to chronicle your joys and flaws,
to save your days from Time's red maw.
Let other local poets prate
of Paris. I say Kirksville's great.

Peabody's Pictorials

The daguerreotypes and cabinet cards abound
with visages Peabody claims are clans
of Jesse James and the Youngers:
he has thousands of these antique images
and no one dares to say he's blundered
in his attribution. Who gives a damn?
He weaves his passionate narrative of found

treasures in flea markets, worth several millions
(the proprietors love to see him coming
across Kansas, Missouri, Iowa).
He spends every last cent from his roofing labors
on these physiognomies, a believer
that these images will set the world humming
and win him the awestruck admiration of billions

of western aficionados. Let him weave his stories
of carnivalesque pop star outlaws,
masqueraders, shape-shifters
who traversed these United States to avoid arrest;
of faked deaths and grifter
aliases assumed for the ignoble cause
of greed, and survival—now Peabody's glories.

Homage to Paris

Remembering James Joyce, Ophelia Parrish classroom, spring 2009

Chariton river
        Anna Livia Plurabelle
                in *Finnegans Wake*.

I saw his death mask
        at Marquette's art museum:
                small elvish genius.

We quenched our deep thirst
        at Shakespeare and Company's
                courtesy fountain.

Hot Left Bank July:
        no cash for first editions
                at this noble shrine.

David Norton's *Police One* in my Media Room

The black youth in profile
leans stoically
like a West African tribal mask;
above his head
another man of color, also with eyes shut,

but in full profile also leans down
to indicate
he takes no joy from this moment.
His brown uniform
suggests a higher rank. But who knows?

All three cops show different colors:
a blue-clad one,
also black, steers the kid into the back
of the squad car;
the only white guy, in grey, can be seen

only by an arm at the left of the frame.
Foucault's always right:
the more power, the less visibility.
In the background
distant car lights shimmer, sinister stars of the Painlands.

Baldwin Hall Bridge

with thanks to Jim Barnes and Guillame Apollinaire

We scurry to and from our classes
        And our loves
     Must I remember them
Pain comes always after joy

Though night comes and the hour chimes
And the days pass away I remain

I gladly grant an override
    To a gal I'd reimburse
        For breast enlargements
Have I come to be this perv

Though night comes and the hour chimes
And the days pass away I remain

Think rather on cedar waxwings
     And Frederic Church sunsets
        Life imitates art
Imitates life above where the railroad once ran

Though night comes and the hour chimes
And the days pass away I remain

Arnie's sticks click no more
      Tom's tobacco tickles nostrils
        no more   where
do they go   return loves

Though night comes and the hour chimes
And the days pass away I remain

Touring Forest Lake

We push off gently
        from the pontoon-besotted marina,
engage the throttle
        still honoring the no-wake zone.
Past the buoys, I let
        her rip. We storm past swimming beach
and petroglyphs.

We slow up in
        the fishing cove, where blue herons
startle us from rushes
        shady. The pilsner tastes fresh
in the steady sun.
        A broken refrigerator's white
punctuation

on the marshy shore
        humbles the view as in Chinese art.
I watch the weeds
        as we return and barrel down
towards the dam,
        past the Point where sunbathers wave.
We sheer past

the concrete spillway
        into the longest bay, aptly named
"Party Cove," with
        kids splashing and margaritas flowing.
The banks veer towards us:
        sunfish leap, propeller mud churns,
Conrad's river runs out.

Another side trip beckons
        to the place where I saw a rattler
stretched canoe's length
        by an intrepid hunter. We pass
a tree of vultures
        overshadowed by (honest) a Stealth bomber
dispatched from Whiteman.

Ominous place indeed . . .
        Then one last detour to "Danger Cove"
with its submerged
        boulders I've met upon occasion.
I round the Point,
        turn off the outboard and coast us
easefully back to dock.

"Got Any Spare Change?"

Ambling down my side of Normal Street
two houses east of Lincoln, I watch
mid-afternoon skateboarders
grind in the road.

"Got any spare change?" a blonde waif who's
wearing a bright purple Guatemalan knit
cap calls. "We need beer money."
I shrug and move on.

Other passers by get squirted with Super Soaker
plastic water blasters or pelted at night with
beer cans or caps by these
teen squatters.

One day I notice two big spurting cocks, curved
lines for jizz spray-painted in turquoise:
one on the front side of the porch,
another of same on

the front of the house behind and above the first.
Scotch in hand, one night Jamie
knocks on their door to learn
the back story:

did they do it in anarchist protest or macho
assertion? No, some mysterious
enemy tagged their home.
Maybe the Beta

Omega Betas, feisty social college women
next door ~ or other high schoolers—
in any case, too much publicity
for the busy street.

They were all driven out of the basement
where they snuck in to sleep
by an absentee landlord
who had enough.

Now our street is quiet again, the house
renovated for rental, taunting graffiti
painted over, unquiet young souls
departed—to where?

Down the Hill to Jim's Funeral Pyre

Sliding down through the new mud made
by tiny leaks in the long green hose,
you arrive at the immense hay field
where hunters once saw a huge alien
mothership block out the stars before it rose
up into chill intergalactic space.

This place has that kind of mojo vibe,
so it is truly fitting and just that here
we will burn the mortal remains of Jim,
who gave up the ghost after long paralysis:
now he reposes on a bier,
wrapped like a mummy in cloth and paste

above a massive pile of native woods
Words are spoken, toasts are raised
before his two sons start the blaze
which jumps up to the top of the tree line
until his body is fully razed.
My fiancée thinks I'm drinking too much

Jack Daniels, caught up in the
Dionysian ecstasy surrounding this fire:
an acknowledgment of Jim's Anglo-Saxon
tastes, the way he wanted this shindig run
after the day he would expire
with family and friends to watch him burn.

Hypocrite lecteur, smile not at our
country customs which offer options
urbanites may not easily endorse or perform.
Such rites can happen on an obscure farm
if the owner has enough gumption
to honor her beloved in such sacral form.

All Yesterday's Dinner Parties

Jim, it's hard to get poems
out of soirées in this town
for me, maybe because I down
too many glasses of wine, play the clown

and forget the evening's lees.
There have been moments, I'll contend
when I never wanted things to end
and didn't have to feign

my happiness: Christiane,
for starters, multi-coursed
and mimicked colleagues all night
to beats of champagne's effervescent delight.

Laura's a great host, too. Her
Thanksgiving dinners make the board groan
with turkey, salads, salsas and pies;
the guest list always yields surprise.

Like Linda's dad, Alzheimer's patient
who followed me to the loo, then halted:
"Young man, I'm behind you for some reason;
I guess I'll know why in due season."

Or the Spanish bohemians who talked
of cyber-art and Bill Burroughs,
declined our cheer—seemingly chastened
by wild days past whose excesses lessened

their fondness for current pleasures.
Or Wallace, clandestine minister
who kept me guessing at his line;
all these made the dinner fine.

Best of all José, Patrick, Matt, Rod
who like to keep the guest list small
for cassoulet and quesadillas
and herbal soups bound to thrill us.

A gourmet restaurant would be nice,
but chefs like these supply the lack
—now that Minn's Cuisine has closed—
with every dish that they propose.

Invocation and Rodeo

The mounted gal trots in carrying our American flag;
we stand and place hands on breast
while singing *The Star-Spangled
Banner*—a severe vocal test
for some whose high notes lag
behind those best
suited to sing
most
here
pressed
into carrying
the burden which drags,
flats and sharps among the rest
of those who constitute the dregs
from rural music classes, those least
qualified to make these sere prairies ring
in fervent song—but whose patriotism is firmest.

And now a nervous rider bolts out of the rusty chute
holding onto a bareback bronco for his very life:
if he lasts eight seconds, there'll be loot;
if not, perhaps a widowed wife.
This brown horse's a beaut
born to cause strife,
a risk not moot:
knife-
like
teeth
arch back at the youth
before he ceases to be upright.
Thrown off for the proverbial loop,
the cowboy waits for the rodeo clown's wiles—
distracting the horse and giving the crowd a laugh
to loosen up this big, increasingly chilly Saturday night
that offers to these spectators a sense of hard-earned worth.

Mormons in the Rain

White shirt, black tie, black pants, black suit:
they travel always in twos
walking or cycling down Normal Street
to make eye contact with you.

They'll cross the street if must needs be
to accost a passer-by
with news of American revelation
that inspires to testify.

Even in a downpour, conversations
can quite readily start;
as steady as the U.S. mail service
they must unburden their hearts.

I've tried to dissuade them occasionally
by saying I know well their books,
or that I'm friends with the local bishops
and a jack who says they're all crooks:

one who even carries the sacred blood
of a founding polygamist.
They seem impressed by such references
and hand me a card in the mist

before they trudge off down the street
and spy another mark;
they'll trundle around to him or her
and keep at it until dark.

Homage

Your
words
free up
my Muse long
locked into criticism,
afraid of the anxiety of influence,
of doing what's been done better before.
Homage threads us out of this labyrinth as Liz
Phair found out when she reinvented *Exile
on Main Street*, for that was not mere
pastiche or "answer song." And,
after all, didn't James Joyce
himself nod to Homer
when *Ulysses*
burst out on
a Paris
day?

The Blue Moon

On Main Street the rain taps down with persistent drip
as Rita and I enter the funky bistro:
I assure her the cheeseburger's worth the trip
although the atmosphere is beyond down low.
Our haggard waitress welcomes us here
and brings us menus and two Miller beers.

We both order said cheeseburger, me with tater tots;
Rita opts for fries, the more traditional choice.
In no time her burger and fries arrive (of the latter there's lots)
as we discuss the graduate program in subdued voice.
I tell her to go ahead and dig into her food:
I'm in no hurry and the cold beer tastes good.

Forty-five minutes later, I begin to wonder:
did they run out of ground beef or buns?
Lacking my food, I suspect a blunder
and ask the waitress, who apologizes: "Hon,
it seems there's been a slight mistake.
The cook dropped your order and went on lunch break."

"Lunch break? He doesn't eat here?" That rings odd,
but the situation's so strange both Rita and I laugh:
"The nerve of some people, honest to God."
Getting more hungry, I order more draft—
Miller Genuine, that is, bottled, not tap.
The Blue Moon's no place for such lagniappe.

Ninety minutes later, my sandwich appears;
despite the long wait, I deem it sublime—
as are the tater tots of memory so dear.
A brief lunch has stretched out for two hours time,
so long the skies have had time to clear
although this overcast day remains drear.

Stormbringer

6/2/2011

Last night, a year after his nocturnal death,
the skies once again blast a windy breath.

Perhaps it's because Arnie played Kent in *Lear*
on a London stage that here

he becomes meteorological avatar
to douse the land with remaining power.

He should have played the king on that stage,
for Arnie too knew how to rage

'Gainst injustice, sham, Washington,
and that nincompoop Bush Sr.'s son—

or what would make him really blaze—
fools who said the Earl of Oxford wrote the plays.

When I got home the next day from work
a cryptic message on my machine did lurk:

sent early morning, its garbled speech
betokened a voice quite out of reach.

Perhaps, like Sun Ra, Arnie can stretch
beyond the confines of murky death:

that undiscovered country kept for souls
who've shuffled off this mortal coil.

After the Parade

7/4/2008

I. Du Kum Inn

After the Shriners' kiddie cars
    drive off eccentrically into
the distance, James, Jimmy, Bob,
    Felix and I decide to peruse

the Du Kum menu and escape the heat.
    The youngsters order pop; the grown-ups beer;
cheeseburgers, onion rings, cajun shrimp
    and tacos readily appear.

The jukebox plays some random tunes
    (Neil Young, Hank Williams, Bob Dylan, the Stones);
James and Bob compare digital photos
    trying to decide which ones

to keep. Other images slumber
    in their non-digital rolls delayed
until developing, both black and white
    and color, carefully framed (even staged)

glimpses of small town life, state
    representatives and democrats,
clowns and beauty queens:
    all the standard cast that

grace parades like this across
    America in every little 'ville today.
Still, this one's our own rendered
    especially in our own way:

lots of candy and throws for the kids,
    making it more like Mardi Gras
than Independence Day; the smart ones
    bring buckets to collect it all.

Everyone gathers at this potlatch:

    the kids get their swag, the shutterbugs
their shots as they blast their rolls,
        politicians garner votes with hugs,

merchants customers. What do the
        beauty queens get in exchange for royal
waves? An assurance, perhaps,
        that their admirers are loyal.

II. My Front Porch

The sun sinks down. Grown-ups relax
        while Felix and Jimmy
seek the big tents with mammoth stacks
        of fireworks for pennies:
bottle rockets which can attack

passing motorists on this day
        of patriotic pride.
Bob shows them how to lay
        the toss with steady stride
to inculcate the best display.

There are close calls. A driver swerves
        in anger at the boys
after one missile's smoky curve
        explodes by him with noise
that jangles his *haut bourgeois* nerves.

Their antics make my street unsafe
        for both the cars and those
on foot. Each red moment they'll strafe
        unwary ones who choose
to wander by and risk their life.

These big booms surely mean something
        as we perform such rites
each year. It's part of why we sing
        anthems on baseball nights:
we still work to slough off the king.

III. City Fireworks

As the sky slowly turns dark,
      we hastily must gather
and look for a place to park
      while all the townies scatter
with the randomness of the Mad Hatter
      in search of the tell-tale mark

of a trajectory from a launch
      of the city's fireworks display.
The jiggling Jello of their paunch
      reveals this task's no play:
they want the best vantage on this day;
      when they find it, a bunch

will gather and watch the sky
      for bursts of purple, magenta, gold—
Chinese genius' lace tracery
      of fire, a spectacle as old
as the Great Wall, controlled
      amazingly by their carefully designed

layering of chemicals which seldom fail.
      We behold these results with delight.
and adults gasp on this noisy night;
      the heavens turn day with all this light
as in our starry dreams we sail

to gather silver apples of the moon,
      not forgetting to swig a beer.
The show has ended all too soon.
      Now we must get out of here
by finding a road that's somewhat clear
      listening to a traveling tune.

For my guests this day's in quotes:
      living the small town *vida loca*
for a few days denotes
      a break in their routine, a hookah
of rural leisure, *très* pukka,
      not a bad time by their litotes.

Before the Deluge

The trees sough in the wind
as my ashen cat gazes out the window:
the darkening sky she seems to mind
as the June temperatures swing low
and the yardbirds small tidbits find

to nourish them pre-storm.
These clouds are Kirksville habitués:
they heralded the '99 cyclone
and watched while I got soaked to the lees
when leaving Paul Mineo's home—

and the day I played at
emulating Henry David Thoreau
and walked to school *sans* umbrella or hat:
I got a drenching so thorough
I looked like a beleaguered wharf rat.

Residents like to pass
away during these frequent tempests;
the storm's grey riders oft amass
and beckon those they deem the best
to leave this tedious life so crass.

Only iced coffee chills my
veins now; it's too early for whiskey or wine
to take off the rainy chill so subtly
and wrap the day in resonance sublime.
So it's only this coffee and poor poetry.

Interlude

The Asian girl (Taiwanese?
Korean?) comes to our
table between rounds

of cool margaritas.
She opens her brown case
of tawdry knotted

bead necklaces, pewter
earrings and faux-jeweled
rings—neatly compartmentalized.

The drunker gals in our group
try these bangles on and
eventually purchase

a bauble or two.
Others find La Pachanga's
management lax to allow this

intrusion into our meal.
Her English won't suffice
to give us a backstory:

is this for charity,
an Asian scholarship
arrangement, or just

a desperate attempt
to get enough money
to pay her rent,

hop on a plane
(or even a bus)
and leave this town

so unpropitious
for solid jobs or
even weak hustles?

Ruth Towne's Bell

What's a campus without a
bell? Emeritus Ruth Towne
concluded naught. So she then
bequeathed funding for Truman
to build a stately tower
to chime the quarter hour
for bustling students to hear
that such a warning in ear
would grant them a burst of speed
and give them the time they need
to make that history class
without appearing an ass.
When finances are tight, though,
you hear the bell sound no more.
Luxury for a public
school, we need a funding trick
to help the bell keep its knoll,
to enable its bright toll
to commemorate a great
lady's gift to Truman State.

Friday Night Concerts on the Square

Charlie Parr strums the piedmont blues
and sings of a man on a riding lawn mower
determined to get his whiskey drink;
the crowds meander relaxed and loose,
stopping to applaud, whistle, yell for more.
As the light dims, their numbers shrink.

Or here comes T.P. as Elvis the King
rounding the square in a white limousine
and handing out to little kids teddy bears—
for some a decidedly perverse thing.
But I say such naysayers are mean:
the youngsters love his fluffy wares.

He belts out "Hurt," "Proud Mary,"
epics like "Suspicious Minds" and "American
Trilogy," and songs Elvis never got to
sing. The mike helps his deep voice carry
for us to rock out as best we can
until his karaoke concert is through.

This square has seen fires and Civil War fights,
anti-nuclear marches, murder trials,
Earth Day concerts with Journey tribute bands.
Now it tolerates these mellower nights
where musicians draw out our deepest smiles,
our tapping feet and claps of callused hands.

Aporia

Small cities seldom organize
their past. No Musee
Carnavalet here
to guide us through scenic stages
where we can solemnly play
at being history.

Kirksville's remnants are in shards:
at Forest Lake, you'll find
petroglyphs from
ancient hands displaying birds and
beasts. Pay no mind
to teen graffiti

which suggests desire for a vulgar
continuity with the past.
Both eras leave their
mark, but we privilege the earlier
Native scribbles over the last
though both technically

defaced the rocks. Or there's
Violette's massive county
history which stops at
nineteen eleven. After the War and the
Cyclone remains much mystery
involving racist re-routing

of train lines and curfews for blacks.
Or so the gossip runs.
A nineteen thirty-nine
silent documentary looks pretty
lily-white. The camera shuns
colored faces, but who

can trust the selected display?
Much more may be offscreen
as always; it's
a question of catering to the
narcissistic ones who stream
into the cinema
to see themselves mirrored back in show.
No signifier from way back then
which does not conceal
as well as reveal. Some historians
would otherwise wish to pretend,
to recapture elusive time.

Betty Ford Died

Now Betty Ford is dead.
Laura got the news on her cell phone:
we raise a glass to drink her home.
Joseph calls her "First-Lady-and-a-Half."
He reasons like a ripe mooncalf:
if the V.P.'s wife is the Second
Lady, and Gerald Ford had the bane

not to be elected President,
"First-Lady-and-a-Half" would be her name—
splitting the difference, diminishing fame.
But Betty still entered our hearts
as a true groundbreaker and woman of parts
upfront about her addictions and facelifts.
We never thought about First Ladies the same

way. To have a clinic named after you
while still alive, a most unusual thing—
one for any modern bard to sing
about. The TV docudrama intervention
scene also riveted our attention.
Who doesn't love a private view
into public lives *sans* strings?

Go little song, and bid her rest
or join her husband in lofty realms—
he who piloted a thankless helm
and gently steered the ship of state
back on course after the great
debacle of Nixon's mess
had left us all so overwhelmed.

The Pink Picnic

    The rainbow banner
covers over the shelter sign
      at Thousand Hills Park.

    Cole's careful manner
lays out paper plates divine:
      Disney princesses, a lark.

    The sun makes us tanner
as we uncover dishes fine
      to nosh on till dark.

    My quinoa pilaf sits
beside sausage and potato treats
      and homemade dill bread.

    Only a few flies flit
among these gorgeous eats
      to surely keep us fed.

    A pink triangle cake fits
where GBLT folks and friends meet
      without fear or dread.

    Our eager mitts
explore designer cupcakes sweet,
      some covered with ants said

    to be chocolate-covered
almonds, or with chrysanthemums neat
      and Legos of candy rare.

    We admiringly hover
over these delicacies replete
      served on a day so fair.

Another American Poet

(just what the world needs . . . really)

The sun bursts out anew
   replacing the gloom
that joined the tornado siren's
   pronouncement of doom
sending me to the basement again.
   Now there's work to do.

Three cats ignore me as I write
   in agon with my counterpart
who wrangled words at the Select
   feeling like Bonaparte—
at least that's what I detect—
   I may not be right.

Do tornadoes ever pummel Paris?
   It seems unlikely at best.
But then Kirksville missed Nazi tanks
   rolling in from the east
and cronkling over the Left Bank:
   advantage for the Midwest.

Neither of us can gain the laurel
   like Eliot, Pound, Lord Byron,
Olsen, Dickinson, Williams, Heaney, Plath;
   still we like to try on
our Muse, walk the stony sacred path,
   maybe point a moral.

Poetry's like carving scrimshaw:
   a delicate, zany pastime
which seldom wins the carver fame
   or earns you one dime,
let alone an immortal name
      before the maggots gnaw.

Le Dialogue au Carmel

for Jo Ann Newman and Carolyn Asp

She glides by,
        blur of
                brocade,
        coming on
            like
            the
            army
                    saxophone experiments.

    Cut the reebop!
            She's
            gone:
            married a
                monkey
                    inna zoo . . .

Clovis Trouille
        micro-mini'd nun,
            I ask you:
                    Why ain't
                    sex
                    a sacrament
        like cigarettes,
                    Scotch
                        or gin?
                            Gnostic twats!

Bataille tells us
        the Earth
            is
            perpetually
                jacking
                off
                    with
                        her
                          tides
                              like a rabid floozy

Commemoration

This town is ruled by Baldwin, Still:
the former has a statue tall,
an academy which will
teach junior high students well
named after him, ditto a hall
and lecture series in the fall.

A.T. Still has a medical
school and museum eponymous
because of methods radical
deployed to try and help us.
Also a gravesite, if that counts,
where cemetery actors mount

a reenactment of the life
(over the July Fourth weekend)
of the osteopath, plus wife,
so his glory might never end.
One town, two great schools: a learning
oasis for those found yearning

for city lights and country air.
Yet Baldwin's backstory's complex:
he wasn't treated quite so fair
by colleagues who gave him the hex,
drove him out—so history books
tell, if you care to give a look.

Now he embodies teacher's ed.,
although none can tell his special
classroom tricks: those who saw are dead,
written memoirs too vague to tell
us much. So Baldwin's a legend,
a pedagogical goad, friend

to all who would teach a good class—
even as Still inspires doctors
and anatomists who amass
to Kirksville for helpful lectures.
Two men extended their great stride
and spread their fame both far and wide.

One O'clock in the Morning

Wending back from Dereck's house at one o'clock
in the morning, from his yard I hear my neighbor's voice
whispering to a guest. I quickly take stock
of this and jokingly tell him to quell the noise,

then mooch a single-malt scotch
off him. We talk of things Minnesotan
with Drew, his son. I drink up, lest I botch
my welcome, and amble home where nought's verboten.

Rod's Way: July 2011

Almost every night I hear the phone
ring sometime after nine. It's Rod
worrying about the health of his mother
or about his romance with the little gal
that prompts him to fix a furtive gin
and sit on the porch to sneak his cigarettes.

He isn't really addicted to those cigarettes,
can stop cold turkey anytime—ditto the gin:
white box wine will suffice if the gal
is on an even keel, even his mother
may let him enjoy a glass in her presence. Rod
can certainly sip wine while he's on the phone

with her. But these days his phone
voice sounds bedraggled. His mother
needs an operation she's far too old a gal
for, which causes a dilemma for Rod,
panic attacks alleviated by Marlboro cigarettes
and the cool, crisp taste of tonic and Gordon's gin.

He likes just a splash of tonic with his gin:
it's called a "Susan" for its inventor, cigarettes
are the perfect accompaniment with it for Rod.
With this shield he can face any gal
or the third-degree queries over the phone
from his nervous, loving mother.

I never had that much contact with my mother—
maybe a good thing. At my best I'd only phone
once a week, avoiding that familial gin.
And only sporadically did I have a gal
who'd share with me marijuana cigarettes.
A completely different world than Rod

inhabits. Quite the fretter is Rod,
and builder of stately German programs which gin
to crumble, a worry in addition to mother
which calls for another pack of cigarettes.
So he assures me over the phone,
a more ready listener than his gal.

Then again, what mother ever concerned a gal
except her own, if that? Gin and cigarettes
direct the right numbers for Rod to punch on his phone.

Heat Advisory

The July heat bakes the street
and makes my tomatoes sun-dried;
the cabbie can wait while I'm at the vet:
no one else wants to ride.

The grass is brown, some leaves are brown
where cicadas emerged and fed;
the wind now and then blows like a sirocco
over this town deserted.

Hoss Jackson's bus caused a little fuss;
he's playing at our fair.
Hoss stopped in for KFC chicken—
to grab some comfort fare.

It'll be hot all week, the weather folks bleat:
be careful with your fun.
Oil up, hydrate, or you won't feel great
beneath this blazing sun.

At the Greek Corner

To savor the fresh gyro
or the juicy Italian beef,
the abundant fries with melted feta,

you must know the ways
of both Chicago and the Aegean.

Poem on Hemingway's Birthday

Today's hotter than your Florida Keys;
I have almost as many cats as you
and drink my pink lemonade to the lees
to give Paul Newman (also gone) his due.

Much tamer than your Paris tipples
or "Death in the Gulf Streams" on your porch,
less likely to send a literary ripple
far and wide ~ or to found a secular church.

With you every American must contend—
nay, every writer who wants to be any good.
Into every language your sentences blend
razor-sharp like well-honed wood.

More than half in love with easeful death,
you offer a way out to some:
an oven sufficed for less macho Plath,
though Hunter wrote "No fun" and followed your gun.

From a flawed life much flawless prose . . .
In other words, art business as usual.
From pain we like to spin our webs—so it goes—
and leave our legacies after the funeral.

I hope you're partying with all those greats
(Fitzgerald, Stein, Pound, Picasso):
fantastic artists and reprobates
who made Twenties Paris shine and pulse so.

Thus, happy birthday, Papa, wherever you are—
or whatever, perhaps, by your own creed.
But I hope you've found a heavenly bar
well-stocked to suit your every need.

Departures

People leave Kirksville for good suddenly
like Pat, according to rampant rumor:
she left much behind, I hear folks murmur,
sold her house, bought a condo in NYC.

This town can freak a person out—
its smallness, its intimacy, its gossip.
You can feel everybody's into your trip
until it just makes you want to shout.

I know this phase, I was there long ago
before I became a near-hermit with my cats,
my books, snake, fish and plants. Now I just

watch the passing show. If you're not
on Facebook, you're out of the main loop
and people leave you alone—as far as you can tell.

As far as I can tell, some folks just don't like
the Midwest. People seem too friendly for some
who want to be left alone in their glum
demeanor. It makes them take amazing hikes

to the United Arab Emirates, a convent, Utah, Phoenix,
Oklahoma. Sometimes we never hear from them again
unless when they left us we were close friends—
otherwise their departure sticks.

Others who were forced to leave for lack of a job,
however, regard this town as a kind of lost Eden.
They return repeatedly and enjoy its low-key

pace and ambience, its modest amenities and
proximity to wild. It's like they never left when they
return, like the bar on *Cheers* where everybody knows

your name. What goes with your name might
be bogus, alas. I've been an Olympic swimmer, a junkie,
gay (of course)—result of misperceptions or unseen irony.
Sooner or later we all look a transgressive fright,

which levels the playing field. Small town folks
eventually ignore these dubious histories, peacefully coexist
as they meet and meet again casually or in a tryst—
or maybe just to share a coffee and some jokes.

We share information, resources, names to hire,
pitch in for a shower or a funeral,
pick up walkers when the days are hot, cold

or wet. We share in each other's triumphs
or sorrows. This happens in Dubai as well,
but here it occurs in concentrated forms.

The concentrated forms of those who gather
to give to the bereaved some solace
unlike anything I've seen in urban populace:
in this town each loss seems to matter.

And we unite around this changing weather:
for all Fox News tries, it fails to convince
us the storms are not getting more intense—
compelling us more often to seek shelter.

My backyard bamboo spreads in some Ballardian world
I've come to know; my kitchen roof leaks now
from the pounding of torrential rains;

cicada-clipped branches swish and twirl
in the counter-rotation of incipient tornado.
The old climates also leave ~ ne'er to be seen again.

I think of my hardest never seen relocations
almost every day: of Arnie, who burned
many a midnight oil while the vinyl turned
till cancer took him to the last station;

or Sue, who brought to my life some glam
with an upgraded abode, love, travel, fun.
In her field they weren't hiring anyone
here, so now I'm Mister Havisham.

These poems remind us of more that's gone:
high modernism's challenging if pompous shards,
the apocalyptic urgency of some free verse

or the epic love for a Maud Gonne.
What remains, comparatively? Hallmark greeting cards
that jingle away while the times get worse.

Formalist poetry tends to jingle away:
the rhyme and meter give a pseudo-vatic voice,
which is why for egomaniacs it's the approach of choice—
not that all poetry doesn't tend this way.

For some that voice is earned, like Komunyakaa or Heaney.
But I also love poetry that mocks pretension
like that of John Ashbery or Carl Martin.
And Jim Barnes, *l'homme moyen sensuel*, holds plenty

of interest for me as you can plainly see.
My verse is blessed and doomed to stand in his shadow—
not by coincidence, but a matter of choice;

it's bound to be a lesser poetry
(to anticipate what every critic will know),
but I hope you, dear reader, still detect a voice.

Dear reader, study your space, rural or urban –
for Patti Smith limned well her Chelsea Hotel
in *Just Kids*. All places have tales to tell
the attentive observer—even landscapes suburban,

which Arcade Fire recollects in nostalgic fury.
It's all poetic grist, like Eliot's rose garden:
write it down so the future can listen.
It's the work and the locale that count—don't worry.

This Sisyphean striving in verse is what we have
to try, certainly, in this remote heartland
(it's how Edgar Lee Masters wrestled eternity);

in these minute particulars we lave
as all around us drifts away like sand,
for people leave Kirksville suddenly.

Midnight in Paris in **Kirksville**

I sip my glass of chilled chardonnay
and munch on
salty, fresh
popcorn

sitting on a comfy upholstered
rocking chair with
an art theatre
full of

dreamers watching lavish
technicolor images
of the City
of Lights.

Our history's different:
a magic transport
would convey us
not to

the Twenties or the
Belle Epoque
but rather
to

a battle or a cyclone—
our impoverished
calamitous
markers.

So we prefer to dream,
even though we've
bet on the
dark

horse. For one Friday
night, Paris and
Kirksville are
sisters.

About Bob Mielke

I was born on November 11, 1954 in Milwaukee, Wisconsin. My mother was a housewife (in the days when that was considered a full-time job); my father was a machinist and electrician for a company that manufactured beer cases for Milwaukee's many—at the time—breweries. He was not eligible for service in World War II, but when I was much older and studying nuclear weapons he revealed to me that he helped build at Allis-Chalmers the giant magnets for separating weapons-grade uranium at Oak Ridge for the Hiroshima bomb. Since my brother worked for the CIA at Area 51 on the Nevada Test Site, nukes have been a recurring theme for the men in my family. My brother and I were first-generation college students from a quintessential blue-collar family that got a great education in Milwaukee's parochial schools.

I grew up in the very serious 'hood of inner-city Milwaukee learning how to shoplift and how to persuade people with guns pulled on me—on my porch and on a city bus, no less—not to use them. The Beatles, Frank Zappa, Neil Young, my sister Pat's Elvis records, Ray Bradbury, Patti Smith, sundry miniskirted nuns (one of whom I went on a group date with in my freshman year of high school!) and the Jesuits helped me to keep moving on up.

I got a great scholarship package to get a PH.D. in English from Duke University back when there was still some greenery between Durham and Chapel Hill. Then I taught for four years full-time and fourteen summers at Wake Forest University, the latter in connection with the Reynolda House Museum of American Art. Every summer we took a field trip to New York, my favorite American city and third favorite overall (preceded by Paris and Toronto: sorry San Francisco, Chicago, London and Marrakesh!). My kitchen to this day has a haunting photo of my summer class atop the World Trade Center one of the many times we got up there. (Someday no young person will know what that's a picture of.)

For the last quarter century I've been teaching at Truman State University (aka Northeast Missouri State University) in English, American Studies and other interdisciplinary fields (including environmental studies). My wackiest courses are on nuclear weaponry, rock and roll and UFOs. The last got funding for a trip to Roswell and the Little Ale E Inn near Area 51. Annie Jacobsen's new book has convinced me that they came from Stalin and Nazi scientists, not Mars.

All those years in Kirksville went into my eponymous first book of poetry. I live with five cats (the legal limit without a kennel license), the oldest of which is 16, and an albino corn snake—in a lovely 1898 carpenter's gothic grey house. I'm still single either because of my lack of a driver's license or because the third arm growing out of my side terrifies women. Or maybe I just haven't met the right (ex-)nun. I hope *Kirksville* the book doesn't make Kirksville the town TOO well-known. To my taste, I wouldn't want us to get much hipper than we are now (as hip as Durham was in 1986).

Who's this Harry Potter everyone's talking about?

Kirksville Bonus Tracks: Q&A with Bob Mielke

Interview conducted, edited and condensed by Kevin C. Fitzpatrick

Jim Barnes, who taught in Kirksville from 1970-2003, was in the same English department with you for more than 15 years. His poetry collection Paris was published in 2007. When did you decide on writing a poem to match each of his, and why?

Necessity is the mother of invention. I'm also completing a huge book on various musical figures like Yoko Ono, Sun Ra, Neil Young and Frank Zappa. I was working on that book in the summer of 2009 and the monitor on my home computer went out. So I couldn't work on the book. But I had an idea percolating for about a year. I was interested in doing this Kirksville book for some time because of reading Paris and also reading Jim Barnes' memoir called *On Native Ground*—without an "s" so he doesn't get it confused with Alfred Kazin's book *On Native Grounds*—and I was astonished in this whole memoir, which is mainly about Europe, Oklahoma, the Pacific Northwest and a few other places, Kirksville got two sentences in the whole book. One saying more or less, "and then I taught for a bunch years at this college in the Midwest" and then one saying, "We had to leave Kirksville for a warmer clime in the winter." And I just thought that this was really astonishing that he gave so much attention to Paris, on somewhat of a tourist level. You'll notice he doesn't get into the depths of characterization that I was able to do. I thought initially Kirksville would be like how Liz Phair did her album *Exile in Guyville* as a song-by-song answer to *Exile on Main Street*.

It was partially for me to say, how come our local poets, with the noteworthy exception of Monica Barron [professor of English at Truman since 1984], don't write about this area? Joe Benevento [professor of English at Truman since 1983] writes about Queens and New York. So I thought I'd correct that. I've been here 25 years. This town deserves to be paid tribute to. I'm tapping into a much larger debate that happened in the early part of the 20th Century between the Continental Modernists like T. S. Eliot and Ezra Pound, and poets of the local like Edgar Lee Masters and his *Spoon River Anthology* and William Carlos Williams' poems about Paterson, New Jersey. And I thought, it's the same old deal, do we write about sophisticated stuff, or do we find the beauty in our everyday lives? That was the side I wanted to take, so when that computer crashed, I decided that until it gets fixed I'm going to work on this other book. So at that point, *Kirksville* went on the front burner and the other book went on the back burner. As I wrote the book it went from being more of a pastiche—it was never a parody of Barnes—but a pastiche where I'm sort of tweaking him for his sort of sophistication, to eventually coming to really respect him. It turned into more of a homage as I wrote. I became really impressed with the difficult verse forms and meters, and rhyme schemes he was working with: just a vast treasure trove. You know, formalist poetry tends to get put down, and I'm not a formalist poet: my next book will definitely be in free verse. This was like handicapping myself a little bit. But the pleasure of working in formal verse is that you can make wonderful discoveries. The music is really great and you get a payoff. It's the difference between playing free jazz and playing within certain recognized changes.

What types of poems did Jim Barnes use? I recognize sonnets, cinquains and triolets. What did you need to learn or adapt to his style?

The funny thing is I did it the way a real idiot would do it. Unless he clued me in, like with "Madrigal" or "Triolet," then I would go online or look up in an encyclopedia of poetics or John Hollander's *Rhyme's Reason: A Guide to English Verse*—a great little book on all the forms—and then I would learn the rules of the game, like learning pig Latin or something. But I found out there were verse forms I was mimicking where I didn't even know what the form was. He has a poem called "Crown" towards the end of his book, and my title is "Departures," and I found out when I read this in Monica Barron's creative writing class when she said, "Oh, you've written a corona." Which, of course, is Latin for "crown". And I said, "What's that, Monica?" And she told me it's a series of linked sonnets, where the last line of the first sonnet is repeated partially in the first line of the second sonnet, and the second in the third, and so on. So I did some forms in here that I didn't even know were forms. I just thought they were interesting ways to write a poem.

I know they are all like your children, but do you have any favorites?

I think I have a different favorite every day. I don't look at my poems every day, but as I was going through the book today to prep for our conversation, I really like, today, "Brashear Park (Within a Budding Grove)." It's about just a really surreal, dare I say Felliniesque—we've been watching Fellini in my film class—moment you get so seldom in life. The setup of the poem is simplicity itself. I had a former student with her son visiting and I live right near Brashear Park. It has a kiddie pool in the summer. I'd seen it when I'd walked by when I was watching someone's dog, but I never really hung out there. And when I went it was this sort of erotic masterpiece. I was the only guy there. There were all these young mothers; some of them were quite extraordinarily beautiful. There was a cute lifeguard. But because I was with my friend and her kid, they didn't immediately write me off as a sexual predator or pervert. So there was that excitement of being a kind of voyeur at a scene that I'd never gotten to participate in before. I don't know if it's the best poem, but to me, it triggers a really interesting memory. And I like the fact that I evoked other poets who write about these kinds of things, like Leonard Cohen in song after song, and I mention W. D. Snodgrass who had a poem called "April Inventory," it's one of the few erotic poems that's tasteful and funny about the desire an aging teacher has in spring for his young female students. It sounds like an awful poem but it's actually quite sad, amusing, wistful and beautiful. So I felt I captured something of that in that poem, along with my big love for Marcel Proust and *A la Recherche du Temps Perdu* (in English, *In Search of Lost Time*). There's a scene in the second volume of *Within a Budding Grove* where he has that experience at a seashore and suddenly sees all these women. It's a busy poem, a lot of them are, but in that one there's a lot of stuff going on. It was triggered by the Barnes poem "Parc de la Turlure." A couple of his poems are about Proust.

Which ones did you labor the most on, or turn over in your mind a lot?

Actually the ones I sent you the variants on. I didn't have a lot of trouble, but "Bequest: *Mi Corazon* to RVM," that one had a couple of endings and I'm glad you picked one for me. And the same thing with the surrealist one, "Le Dialogue au Carmel." That's actually the only poem in the book where there's an earlier poem of mine recycled that was never published. I wrote the first half of that poem in 1975 or 1976. When I was in New York one summer I saw Clovis Trouille's painting "Le Dialogue au Carmel"—which gives the poem its title—of nuns hiking up their skirts and smoking cigarettes. It's really an astonishing painting. They had to drag me away from it after I was there for about 90 minutes looking at it. They thought I was trying to find a way to get past the electronic monitoring system and sneak it out of the Guggenheim.

"The Confederate Army Field Hospital" and "Cemetery Theatre" are two of my favorites, and they are also about Kirksville history, which figures into the work, particularly Civil War history and 19th Century founders/educators. The city can't match Paris for history, but it does have quite a colorful past.

It really does. Centering on the two big events I found out from reading the 1100-plus page *History of Adair County* [written by Eugene Morrow Violette, published in 1911] were the Civil War battle and what they call "The Cyclone" [it struck April 27, 1899, and killed nearly 40]. In fact, you can go to the Square and those are the plaques that they decided to commemorate. Those are the big things. Then you have funky activity with Mormons and a few other tidbits. But those two are the real big points; I had to make a lot of use of them, because as you say, Paris, France, has a lot more to talk about.

What did you like researching or learning about the most to write these poems?

Probably the most interesting thing I looked at, and it shows up in the poem "Aporia," is the result of the Adair County Historical Society finding a 1930s film. An itinerant film company would go through little towns in the Midwest and they would make a movie with everybody in town in it, at their jobs or doing recreational things. It's about 90 minutes long and it was shown in the local theater. So people would, in effect, pay to see themselves, with a piano accompaniment. They found this thing and I got a copy, and it was really helpful because Violette's History ends in 1911. A music professor here, David Nichols, recently put out *Founding the Future: A History of Truman State University*, about Truman in all its many incarnations. So we have that. But there was a big gap from 1911 to the present for the city. So this piece of material history really helped me kind of see an interconnecting story. It also raised a lot of questions; that's what the poem is about. Any historical artifact conceals as well as reveals, because I didn't see any black faces in the entire 90-minute film. I really found myself wondering about that. There are some records that they passed "sundown" legislation in the Twenties, and that's why the train station is in La Plata and not Kirksville, to keep the "riff raff" from coming up. But I thought surely there must be some working as cooks or servants, but you don't see them. They're not in the frame. That to me was as interesting as what was in the frame.

Many of the poems in Kirksville mention your friends, townspeople and fellow teachers. But you also recall friends you were close to such as Arnie Preussner, who you taught with for 20 years, who have passed away. In "Near Arnie's House," "Stormbringer," and "Departures"—what should readers know about him that isn't in the poems?

They should look at his book. Just before he died he published, *Replaying the Renaissance*, it's a mix of Shakespeare and Ben Jonson, whom he did his PhD on, and his deep interest in film. His essays comparing Woody Allen's *The Purple Rose of Cairo* to its Shakespearean sources, and all that cool stuff. So he was a fine scholar. And also he was just one of the nicest people I ever hung out with. When he was in good health—and even when he wasn't— we'd get together every Friday night. We'd start out officially with drinks and dinner at the DuKum Inn and the downtown area. Then we'd come back to my place, and we might watch one movie, we might watch two movies. Usually his wife, Alanna, would go home and then we'd start spinnin' the vinyl. And that could go until four in the morning, easily. He liked to drink, but he never got drunk. He was one of the most loyal people; once you made a friendship with him you had a friend for life. He really cared about his teaching, but he always put himself down as a teacher: he didn't think he was a very good teacher. I actually took a class from him. I thought, "I've got to see, he can't be as bad as he says," and it was one of the best classes I ever took. We did a nice road trip with a class; it was a grad seminar on Jacobean drama. We went up to Stratford, Ontario, to see some Shakespeare plays. Arnie was a really well-rounded individual; he was pretty much interested in everything. So we hit it off the minute I met him. I was on the interview team, and ironically, he was told by the guy doing the hiring, "We have a really great faculty, except for this weirdo, Bob Mielke."

I was particularly moved by "2404 North East Street," which is about another faculty member who died, Tom Coates, in June 2009.

That was really sad and it was a bad death, for a number of reasons. One being that his family did not want any memorial. My brother did the same thing when he died; in the will he said no memorial. Tom didn't have any say in it; he didn't request that, that was his family's choice. I think the living need closure with something like that. So this poem, in its own modest way, gives people some closure on Tom's death that they didn't get from the family. He was a really brilliant and fun Spanish professor. He socialized comfortably with his students. He became a kind of go-to guy. We have a lot of difficult teachers here, and I think it's really important at every university that there be a back door. Tom was like the Underground Railroad to the Spanish requirement while he was alive and teaching. That was a good thing because Spanish is the most popular language. I'm a realist. I taught freshman writing last fall; some people just want to get through the requirement. I had students who said, we're going to be scientists, we don't ever want to write again, we just want to work in labs. So different strokes for different folks, and Tom really had a market niche. He was an incredible cook and a very entertaining guy to be around.

What can you say about Karl Kopitske, who is in "Triolet For Karl" and "Three Deaths" that readers won't know?

That was really tragic. He was a great guy. I went to Hawaii with him. He was a wonderful student, undergrad and grad. Big guy, red hair, people got him confused with the singer from Simply Red, whenever he went into a bar. And at age 35 [according to the obituary; I was told he was 33] he just died of a heart attack. Just boom. No indication, whatsoever. They found in the autopsy he had over 70-percent blockage in his arteries. He was completely primed for it but there were no warning signs; it was heredity. Karl was fascinating; he was a missionary kid who grew up in Papua New Guinea. We had some mighty good times together. He got the grad students to do a marathon 72-hour poetry reading on the campus to buy a school bus. Which we did.

Your poem "The Trip to Bountiful" is about Geraldine Page. Is she the only movie star born in Kirksville?

Yes, to my knowledge and my research. The only one yet. The key is "born" because we have others. Jenna Fischer went to Truman, but that doesn't count. But born in Kirksville, given the size of the town, there might be some minor bit player, I don't know. Most people don't even know Geraldine Page was born here; I only found out because I saw a movie she was in and really liked it. I looked her up and found she was from Kirksville. Amazing.

The poems also mark some of the high points in your life in Kirksville. Would you say spending time with Susan Sontag ranks up there?

Oh absolutely. The other issue I'd point out is because I'm following Jim: some of his poems are about meeting minor celebs and stuff like that. So to match his poems I definitely wanted to dip into that. Yeah, every minute with Sontag was memorable. She's one of these people, you have a lot of them living in Manhattan, where they wake up and they're on, and they're on all day. Susan Sontag, I'm sure, even in her downtime, she would read a book. But she was always go, go, go, go, go. She made me see Kirksville through new eyes. She really appreciated it. She wanted to do things like go to the osteopathy museum and see the human nerve system, all that stuff. She had done her homework before she came here.

How did Toons [a local honky tonk dance place] and Sontag come together in "Looking For Sontag's Ghost at Toons"?

I took her to Toons, yep. I tried not to tell a single lie in the entire book. It went just as it went down. When she got into her beer she started talking about hanging out with John Lennon and Yoko Ono, she danced with the cowboys. And she was pretty astonishing. She was over six feet tall, white shock of hair on a dyed-black mane. What was really weird, and it's not in the poem, is that two years later I took students from Wake Forest up to New York and we went to the "Mostly Mozart" concert at Lincoln Center. I ran into her and she went, "Hi Bob, how're you doing?" She remembered me, so I thought that was pretty cool.

Two of your recurring themes are music and fireworks.

What's great about fireworks is that in Kirksville, fireworks are unconditionally legal from late June to about July 7. Or a couple days after the Fourth. Then it's like Bourbon Street at Midnight on Shrove Tuesday; they shut everything down and you get seriously busted if you light one off. But during that time I think you could probably get something approaching a tactical nuclear weapon and detonate it, if you had the right place to do it. So I go nuts. I'm a pyromaniac, as was Karl. I easily spend $600 to $1000 a year on fireworks. I don't mess with anything that's less than 50 bucks; you really want the industrial strength ones. And you want to find a farm. I once did it in Brashear Park for a wedding ceremony, and they changed the regulations I think because of me. But my backyard, forget about it, I would cause huge amounts of fire. But on a farm, especially if the weather conditions are right and it's not too dry, usually it isn't, it's just amazing. The city does a really good job too. But a little bit of boasting here, my display is almost as good as the city's. The city throws a lot of money at it.

Music too, it's the other book I'm writing, but music is a major food group in my life. I don't just use it as background, I like to put it on and really listen to it. Part of that is being trained by teaching American Studies at Wake Forest with Louis Goldstein, a really good music professor who taught me how to listen to music and appreciate it. One of my great regrets is I never learned. I mean, I can noodle on keyboards and percussion, but I never really studied music. It's one of the great regrets of my life; I think that train has left the station. I have a lot of friends, like Bill McKemy, a jazz player, who are musicians and I like to talk about music with musicians. In a way this new book is going to be trying to write about music for non-specialists.

"All Yesterday's Dinner Parties" is close to "Departures . . ."

Yeah, everybody likes my "All Yesterday's Dinner Parties" because I name-check so many people and cooks. One of the things that poem points out, one of the greatest losses I'd say, culinarily, in my years here in Kirksville was the closing of Minn's Cuisine. There's nothing that substitutes for that. But people have stepped up to the plate; I happen to know some of the finest cooks I've ever dined with, so we do have a lot of great cooking. "Departures" is based on "Crown" in *Paris*, what's interesting is that, it's the longest poem in the collection, and it touches so many bases. It goes into people's ambivalence about the Midwest, especially people not from the Midwest. Eventually it gets to the issues of loss and the meaning of art.

Let me ask you about a theme in those two poems. What's it been like for 25 years to see friends, faculty and students come and go to Kirksville, and you stay there, carrying on. How do these poems collectively sum up the city, and living there?

It's a transient population. People do come back. It's really interesting, and "Departures" sort of hints, for some people they can't wait to shake the dust from their feet. I'd say there are two patterns, some people leave Kirksville and they never want to talk about it again. They don't give you their forwarding e-mail. They're gone. Then there are other people who really miss it and keep coming back. I have a friend and colleague in St. Louis, she said that if she won the Powerball she'd buy a house here, and move, immediately. She prefers Kirksville to St. Louis on every count. There is that thread, but as you get older you see the deaths. The other thread that is in counterpoint to that is the weather keeps getting crazier. If anyone doubts climate change is a reality and thinks Al Gore is blowing smoke, they should come here. It's amazing... if you chart it on a graph it's like an accelerating curve. We've had more tornados in the Midwest and the Southeast in the last week than we've had in whole seasons. The local weather folks are telling us to buy a hardhat, you're going to need it.

You say "In My Library, A Promise" you write you'll never leave Kirksville.

Yeah. That would be a lie if I did then, right? I'll certainly visit other places, and have, but I really like my house. It's a really great 1898 carpenter's gothic. I'm looking at the economic realities of where one can move. You have to ask yourself the hard questions. And going back to the weather issue, the climate will be like New Mexico by the time I retire. It's going in that direction. It's a very comfortable place to live. I love the proximity of Thousand Hills State Park and the way nature's all around. And that's true in New York; of course, you've got your wonderful Central Park. But I can be having breakfast and look up and see a hawk looking in on my cats, wanting to figure out a way to get into the house and get 'em. There's Canadian geese going by, a block away there's a great horned owl that hoots at night by the bed and breakfast. And occasionally you can hear a scream when the owl catches some prey. That wasn't like growing up in Milwaukee or the cities in North Carolina. It's a very different thing here.

You also say in "No Direction Home," that, "If you live here ten years, you'll be a local, but you'll never be a townie."

Right. And I get that totally. It was kind of the same deal in North Carolina. People were very friendly with the much-fabled southern hospitality. But it was also really clear that in the South—especially if you had the bad taste to be a Yankee—your grandkids have a shot at being considered locals, as opposed to an outsider who they're polite to. So Kirksville's a tough nut to crack. That quote is accurate, I am a local, but I'm not a townie. You might even say to yourself in a way that's a good thing, I don't know if I want to be one. There are some aspects of townie culture that are kind of problematic.

Violette's *History of Adair County* **was written in 1911. Say in 100 years, someone picks up Kirksville. You and I and everyone else in the book will be long gone. What would you want someone in 2112 to know about Kirksville?**

I would hope what they got from reading the book was that there's some variety. This is not a monolithic existence. In fact, Kirksville's gotten much more sophisticated from when I got here 25 years ago. By leaps and bounds. The revolutions were UPS deliveries and the Internet. I used to go to cities and carry these huge suitcases full of books, records and media that I'd bought. Now we're going towards Kindle and Netflix, it's a whole other world. Kirksville is as plugged in, in its own strange way, as anywhere else. That's really been a revolution. I think if you juxtapose this book with the Violette *History* you'll see that sure wasn't the case. It was a very different world. Kirksville is globalized. Giving what I'm talking about meteorologically, the weather poems will be interesting. Who can imagine what the weather will be like in 100 years? Kirksville will be a desert, there will be cacti, you know? They'll be wondering about that, they'll say, "Wow, this place used to get rain?" Who knows? History is a mixture of resonance and wonder. I'm borrowing this from a really great historian and theorist, Stephen Greenblatt. The example I give is Mount Vernon, George Washington's home. When I went there, they used to let you sit—they don't anymore—on the huge front porch facing the Potomac, in rocking chairs. And we had this picnic lunch in these. And I thought, this is resonant. This could be my porch, but it's just a bigger porch. And then there's the wonder: the wild, Federalist eye-popping colors. And of course the slave quarters; things are just so different. And I think anyone that reads about the past, that's kind of the tension.

Some things in this book I confidently predict the reader will say, "Oh, we do that too." And other things will be, "Really? You guys did this? Fireworks were legal?" You don't know, but the future will be a surprise. I really do think the Du Kum will be here in 100 years. That's one of the few things I'm confident about. If I were betting on it, the Du Kum and the courthouse will be there. And probably Pancake City.

www.ingramcontent.com/pod-product-compliance
Ingram Content Group UK Ltd.
Pitfield, Milton Keynes, MK11 3LW, UK
UKHW041958230426
12048UKWH00008B/402